OUR
GREAT
STATES

WHAT'S GREAT ABOUT
LOUISIANA?

✳ Rebecca Felix

LERNER PUBLICATIONS ✳ MINNEAPOLIS

CONTENTS

Content Consultant: Sharlene Sinegal DeCuir, Assistant Professor of History, Xavier University of Louisiana

Lerner Publications Company
A division of Lerner Publishing Group, Inc.
241 First Avenue North
Minneapolis, MN 55401 USA

For reading levels and more information, look up this title at www.lernerbooks.com.

Main body text set in ITC Franklin Gothic Std Book Condensed 12/15.
Typeface provided by Adobe Systems.

Library of Congress Cataloging-in-Publication Data

Felix, Rebecca, 1984–
    What's great about Louisiana? / Rebecca Felix.
        pages cm. — (Our great states)
    Includes index.
    Audience: Ages 7–11.
    ISBN 978-1-4677-3879-8 (lb : alk. paper)
    ISBN 978-1-4677-8503-7 (pb : alk. paper)
    ISBN 978-1-4677-8504-4 (eb pdf)
    1. Louisiana—Juvenile literature. I. Title.
F369.3.F45 2015
976.3—dc23   2014045362

Manufactured in the United States of America
1 – PC – 7/15/15

LOUISIANA Welcomes You!

Welcome to Louisiana! It is the land of swamps, spicy seafood, and swinging jazz music! There is a lot to celebrate. Louisiana is the heart of the Cajun and Creole cultures. Cajun dancing is a blast. Blues, zydeco, jazz, and other types of music fill city streets and backwoods bayous. There are many fun activities to explore in Louisiana's sizzling hot weather. Tour a swamp to see alligators up close. Or watch a Civil War reenactment. Read on to learn about ten things that make Louisiana great!

Welcome to Louisiana

Bienvenue én Louisiane

Explore Louisiana's cities and all the places in between! Just turn the page to find out about the PELICAN STATE. >

NEW ORLEANS

> New Orleans is a city known for fun! Ready to explore? Go behind the scenes at Mardi Gras World. It is a glimpse into the world-famous festival! See the giant floats and the props and the statues that decorate them. Some are shaped like dragons or alligators. Try on costumes covered in feathers and glitter.

Next, board a historic streetcar to the Audubon Zoo. Visit the zoo's biggest beasts: dinosaurs! Giant dino robots move and roar. Then grab a wet suit and dive into the zoo's aquarium. Snorkel with fish and float past coral. Are you hungry after your swim? Stop by the Insectarium Bug Appétit Buffet at the Audubon Butterfly Garden and Insectarium. Here chefs create dishes out of edible bugs. The Audubon Butterfly Garden and Insectarium is one of the largest insect museums in North America! View live butterflies and models of prehistoric insects.

Ready to end the day with something spooky? Gray Line's Ghosts & Spirits Walking Tour begins at 7:30 p.m. Visit some of the city's spookiest spots. Your guide will share terrifying tales about the spirits that haunt them.

MARDI GRAS

Mardi Gras in New Orleans began in the 1700s. It was a time to celebrate before a forty-day religious fast each spring. The festivities became a big part of New Orleans culture. These days, people come here from around the world. They watch the parades of colorful floats. Some people dress in elaborate and colorful costumes.

NE KERN'S
GRAS WORLD
ORLEANS, LA.

The Audubon Butterfly Garden and Insectarium is full of bugs!

7

SWAMP TOURS

> Did you know that nearly two million alligators live in Louisiana? A visit wouldn't be complete without meeting some. Take a swamp boat tour with Jean Lafitte Swamp Tours in Marrero. Egrets, wild boars, and nutria walk the shores. Keep an eye on the murky water. What looks like a log might be a gator! Watch for slithering tails and scales. Gators feed, swim, and stare you down. There's even a baby gator on board! Hold it if you're feeling brave.

Float just inches away from gators and feed them from your tour boat on a Cajun Encounters Honey Island Swamp Tour in Slidell. Take a spooky night tour. You won't know how many gators surround you until the lights shine! Try not to jump when you see a gator right next to the boat.

LOUISIANA WETLANDS

Wetlands include swamps, marshes, and bayous. They are very important to the region. Wetlands hold great amounts of water and nutrients. Wetlands also prevent shoreline erosion. Animals such as shrimp, oysters, and birds live in wetlands. Many of these creatures could not survive anywhere else. Larger animals in the wetlands' food chain, such as muskrats and falcons, depend on these smaller animals to live.

You can see alligators up close on a Cajun Encounters Honey Island Swamp Tour.

BATON ROUGE

> The USS *Kidd* Veterans Museum in Baton Rouge allows you to step back in time and explore a real World War II (1939–1945) ship. The USS *Kidd* was a US Navy destroyer. Climb into the ship's belly and stay for an overnight adventure. You can leave your gear in the sailors' bunks. Take a nighttime tour to learn more about sailor life. Listen to stories about historic battles! But be sure to go right to sleep at lights-out. At six thirty the next morning, it's time to wake up, pack up, and head out. Sailors have to follow the rules at sea!

Don't leave Louisiana's capital city without touring its beautiful historic buildings. Visit the Old Louisiana Governor's Mansion. It was built in 1930 as a copy of the White House. Louisiana's Old State Capitol looks like a castle. Which building is your favorite?

The Old Louisiana Governor's Mansion (*left*) and Louisiana's Old State Capitol (*right*) are fun buildings to explore!

FAMOUS FESTIVALS

Hold a frog (*above*) and try frog legs (*below*) at the Rayne Frog Festival.

> Louisiana is famous for its festivals. Celebrate crawfish, or mudbugs, at Mudbug Madness. It's held each May in Shreveport. Get ready for crustacean fun! Pick a live crawfish to enter in a race. Cheer your mudbug on! Then sign up for the kids' crawfish-eating contest. Make sure you're hungry! The first kid to finish 3 pounds (1 kilogram) of crawfish within thirty minutes wins!

Next, visit the Rayne Frog Festival in Rayne. The frogs wear clothes! Which will win the best-dressed frog competition? Enter a frog in a race or a jumping contest. Don't leave the Frog Capital of the World without tasting one of these delicious critters. Frog legs are a Louisiana favorite!

SCI-PORT

> Where can you find out how much you'd weigh on the moon? Where could you watch a shark dissection? Check out Shreveport's science center, Sci-Port! It has a space center, a planetarium, and an IMAX theater.

Want to investigate a crime scene? Maybe you'll do chemistry experiments with Thanksgiving foods. You can even find out what makes fireworks explode! Need a rest after all that science? Lie down on a bed of approximately three thousand nails! Don't worry, they won't pierce you. And you'll find out why not.

Pack for a themed overnight camp-in. You might go on a pirate quest. Or you could end up lost in space! Movies play after lights-out for campers who want to stay up all night.

Learn all about the planets and the universe at Sci-Port.

NEW ORLEANS MUSIC FESTIVALS

> Louisiana is filled with music. Fun festivals let visitors experience jazz, blues, zydeco, and more Louisiana-style music.

Thousands of people attend the New Orleans Jazz & Heritage Festival. Ten days of concerts and fun make up the festival each spring. Sway to the sounds of blues. Swing to jazz. Then check out the marketplace. Watch craftspeople make swamp boats, drums, accordions, and more. You can even learn how to knit your own shrimp net!

Every April, people pack the city for the French Quarter Festival. Watch a New Orleans brass band parade. It's a second-line parade. That means you can join in and boogie! Then head to the riverfront kids' area. Snack on alligator sausage po'boys or turtle soup. Check out the children's performance tent. Kids can make music too! Learn to play in a jazz band. Then perform for family and friends.

THE HISTORY OF JAZZ

In the 1800s, there were many styles of music in New Orleans, including Creole music and slave music. Over time, they blended into a new music style: jazz. Jazz emerged in the early 1900s. Many musicians improvised songs. Jazz was new, expressive, and fun. People played jazz at city picnics. They played at fish fries and in parades. The music style's popularity grew. Jazz has been a part of Louisiana culture ever since.

Try out a po'boy sandwich at a New Orleans music festival!

BATTLEFIELD REENACTMENTS

> Imagine standing in the middle of an American Civil War (1861–1865) battle. Bullets whiz through the air. The ground shakes. Cannons fire. Smoke floats over the battlefield. You don't need to travel back in time. Just visit Louisiana!

The Siege of Port Hudson (1863) lasted more than six weeks. Yearly reenactments fit the battle into one weekend each March. Soldiers march and fire their muskets. You may wander through the camps and become part of the scene. Ask soldiers about their lives. They will answer as real Civil War soldiers would!

The Battle of Pleasant Hill (1864) was one of the largest Civil War battles west of the Mississippi River. Hundreds of people reenact it each April. Salute soldiers as they march in a parade. Watch them battle with cannons and muskets. Wait for the smoke to clear. Then examine covered wagons and tents close up. Craftspeople, medics, and soldiers will answer all your questions. What was camp food like? How were wounded soldiers cared for? Were battles scary?

THE CIVIL WAR IN LOUISIANA

In 1861, many southern states left the Union, or the United States, to start a new group called the Confederacy. Many Louisianans wanted to stay in the Union at first. But Abraham Lincoln had been elected president. Lincoln, a northerner, was against the expansion of slavery. Most Louisianans supported slavery. Lincoln's election caused many Louisianans to change their minds about the Union. Louisiana seceded, or left the Union, in January 1861. It was the sixth state to do so. Many Louisianans went on to fight in the Civil War.

Think of some questions for the reenactors. What do you want to know about life during the Civil War?

CAJUN AND CREOLE CELEBRATIONS

Check out the crafts and get your face painted at the Festival International de Louisiane.

> The city of Lafayette is home to three fun Cajun and Creole fetes. Learn Cajun and zydeco dance moves at the Festival Fête de Famille. Listen to young performers. Family bands play fiddle, accordion, guitar, and violin.

Next, head to the concerts of Festivals Acadiens et Créoles. Show off your new moves! The spicy smells of Cajun and Creole dishes float in the air. Try some traditional foods. Be sure to wipe your face afterward! You'll need it clean for face painting at the festival's La Place des Petits. Join games and make crafts.

The Festival International de Louisiane is a spring celebration of Louisiana's French, Caribbean, Hispanic, and African cultures. Watch street performers. Some walk on stilts. Count the colors in their bright costumes! Learn to play the French game pétanque. Then sign up for the pétanque tournament. Before you leave, try out cool robotics that let you play an interactive music video game!

THE CAJUN PEOPLE

Cajun comes from the French words *les Acadiens*. Acadians were people who settled in Louisiana. They were forced to leave Canada in the 1700s. Cajuns have their own musical sound that consists of a blend of accordions and string instruments, including the fiddle. Cajun food dishes combine local ingredients, such as shrimp and pork sausage, and spices.

SAFARIS

Birds will flock to the birdseed on your stick in the parakeet enclosure at Gone Wild Safari.

> Have you ever petted a giraffe's nose? What about feeding a zebra out of your hand? You can do both in Louisiana! Thousands of animals roam free at the Global Wildlife Center in Folsom. Your safari wagon will take you right up to them! Buy animal feed to get ready for wild encounters. Deer, antelope, zebra, longhorn cattle, and giraffes live together here. See them all up close when they approach the wagon windows. They'll nuzzle, nibble, and slurp up snacks from your hands. You may also spot kangaroos, exotic birds, and giant turtles.

Want to get even closer? Head to Gone Wild Safari in Pineville. Ostriches, bongo, elk, and other animals come right to your open bus window! After the tour, grab a stick covered in birdseed. Head into the parakeet enclosure. Dozens of these tiny birds fly around. One might land on your stick. It wants a bite of birdseed. Next, visit smaller animals at the petting zoo. Or search for small trinkets at the mining center. You get to keep any gold, gems, and fossils you find!

Deer lock horns at the Global Wildlife Center in Folsom.

ABITA MYSTERY HOUSE

> The Abita Mystery House in Abita Springs is a museum full of weird and unexplained items. Are you interested in scary, scaly creatures? You will see evidence of the Honey Island Swamp Monster. The museum has a mold of the monster's footprint. Get ready to be amazed!

Stand next to Buford the Bassigator. He's a fish-gator sculpture the size of a school bus! There's also a display of a strange miniature town. What do the buttons do? They make the town come alive! One button starts up a tiny barbecue. Head outside to examine the House of Shards next. The entire building is coated in thousands of broken bits of glass, pottery, and other sharp pieces. Also outside is a silver trailer that sits in the woods. It looks like a UFO crashed into it!

YOUR TOP TEN

You've just learned about ten things that make Louisiana great. If you were making a list, what activities would you include? What places in Louisiana sound most fun? Write down your top ten choices. Then turn your list of choices into a book just like this one! Search for images of Louisiana online or in magazines. Cut them out or print them to add to your book. Or draw your own pictures!

ON THE INTERNET UCMMUSEUM.COM

INQUIRE HERE FOR CAREER COUNSELING

SHOP IN HERE

XIT HERE

Zero-Volt

The dioramas, including this one of Mardi Gras, come to life at the Abita Mystery House.

Buford the Bassigator lives in a 26-foot (8-meter) shed outside the Abita Mystery House.

LOUISIANA BY MAP

> MAP KEY

⊛ Capital city

○ City

⬡ Point of interest

▲ Highest elevation

—·— State border

UNION JUSTICE AND CONFIDENCE

Visit www.lerneresource.com to learn
more about the state flag of Louisiana.

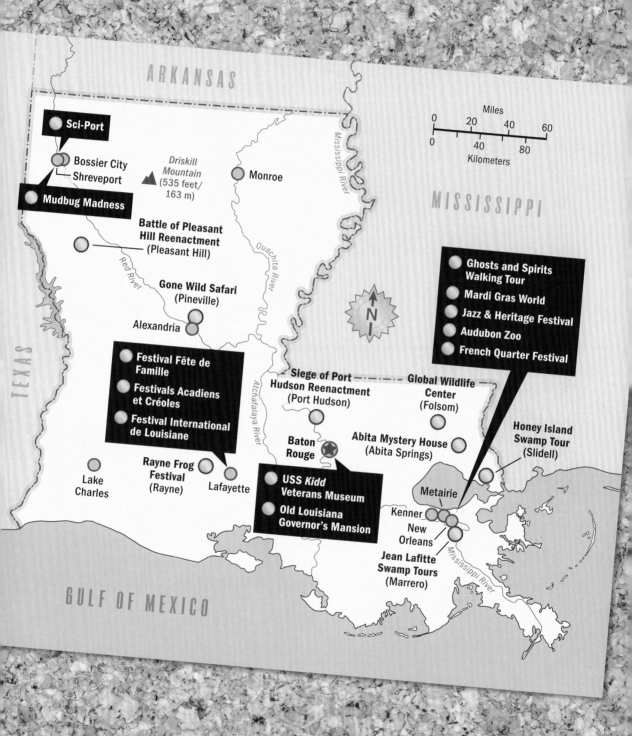

ARKANSAS

Sci-Port

Bossier City
Shreveport

Driskill
Mountain
(535 feet/
163 m)

Monroe

MISSISSIPPI

Mudbug Madness

Battle of Pleasant
Hill Reenactment
(Pleasant Hill)

Ouachita River

Gone Wild Safari
(Pineville)

Red River

Alexandria

Ghosts and Spirits
Walking Tour

Mardi Gras World

Jazz & Heritage Festival

Audubon Zoo

French Quarter Festival

Miles

0   20   40   60

0   40   80

Kilometers

N

TEXAS

Festival Fête de
Famille

Festivals Acadiens
et Créoles

Festival International
de Louisiane

Atchafalaya River

Siege of Port
Hudson Reenactment
(Port Hudson)

Global Wildlife
Center
(Folsom)

Honey Island
Swamp Tour
(Slidell)

Baton
Rouge

Abita Mystery House
(Abita Springs)

Rayne Frog
Festival
(Rayne)

Lake
Charles

Lafayette

USS Kidd
Veterans Museum

Old Louisiana
Governor's Mansion

Metairie

Kenner

New
Orleans

Mississippi River

Jean Lafitte
Swamp Tours
(Marrero)

GULF OF MEXICO

LOUISIANA FACTS

NICKNAME: The Pelican State

SONGS: "Give Me Louisiana" by Doralice Fontane and "You Are My Sunshine" by Jimmie H. Davis and Charles Mitchell

MOTTO: "Union, Justice, and Confidence"

> **FLOWER:** magnolia

TREE: bald cypress

> **BIRD:** brown pelican

ANIMAL: Louisiana black bear

DATE AND RANK OF STATEHOOD: April 30, 1812; the 18th state

> **CAPITAL:** Baton Rouge

AREA: 47,632 square miles (123,366 sq. km)

AVERAGE JANUARY TEMPERATURE: 50°F (10°C)

AVERAGE JULY TEMPERATURE: 82°F (28°C)

POPULATION AND RANK: 4,625,470; 25th (2013)

MAJOR CITIES AND POPULATIONS: New Orleans (378,715), Baton Rouge (229,426), Shreveport (200,327), Lafayette (124,276), Lake Charles (74,024)

NUMBER OF US CONGRESS MEMBERS: 6 representatives, 2 senators

NUMBER OF ELECTORAL VOTES: 8

> **NATURAL RESOURCES:** forests, natural gas, oil

AGRICULTURAL PRODUCTS: chicken, corn, cotton, pecans, potatoes, rice, soybeans, sugarcane, sweet potatoes

MANUFACTURED GOODS: chemicals, metal products, processed foods, processed petroleum and coal, transportation equipment

STATE HOLIDAYS AND CELEBRATIONS: Mardi Gras

GLOSSARY

bayou: a stream that runs through a swamp and connects to a lake or a river

crawfish: a crustacean that looks like a lobster and lives in rivers and streams. It is also called a crayfish.

edible: able to be eaten

erosion: the wearing away of land by water, wind, or ice

fast: when people stop eating food or certain foods for a certain amount of time

fete: a large party or celebration

nutria: a large rodent with webbed hind feet that lives in Louisiana swamps

pétanque: a French game played by throwing metal balls as close as possible to a wooden ball

reenactment: an event at which actors perform the actions of an earlier event

secede: to formally leave a group or an organization

second line: a group of people who follow musicians in a New Orleans brass band parade just to dance to the music

wetland: an area of land covered in shallow water

zydeco: lively music that originated in southern Louisiana and has French and Caribbean roots

FURTHER INFORMATION

America's Story: Explore the States—Louisiana
http://www.americaslibrary.gov/es/la/es_la_subj.html
Check out pictures, maps, videos, and stories about Louisiana musicians, cultures, Mardi Gras, and more.

Freedman, Jeri. *Louisiana: Past and Present*. New York: Rosen Central, 2011. Read about Louisiana's past and how it has influenced the modern state's people, cultures, and economy.

Learning Games for Kids.com: Louisiana State Symbols Games
http://www.learninggamesforkids.com/us_state_games/louisiana
Solve puzzles and play all types of games about Louisiana topics, including state animals and terms, the flag and state symbols, festivals, and Cajun and Creole cultures.

Owings, Lisa. *Louisiana*. Minneapolis: Bellwether Media, 2014. Learn more about the geography and culture of Louisiana.

Thibodeaux's Treasure
http://lacoast.gov/new/Ed/KidsCorner/TT/Default.aspx
Explore Louisiana's wetlands by playing this interactive game. Earn stickers at each level to complete a colored state seal!

Wojahn, Rebecca Hogue, and Donald Wojahn. *An Estuary Food Chain: A Who-Eats-What Adventure in North America*. Minneapolis: Lerner Publications, 2010.
Travel through the swamp and learn about its animals, including what they eat and how they hunt for food.

INDEX

PHOTO ACKNOWLEDGMENTS

The images in this book are used with the permission of:
© CBD/iStockphoto, p. 1; NASA, pp. 2–3; © Laura Westlund/Independent Picture Service, pp. 4, 27; © Katherine Welles/Shutterstock Images, p. 5 (top); © Simply Photos/Shutterstock Images, p. 5 (bottom); © Nick Higham/Alamy, pp. 6–7; © American Spirit/Shutterstock Images, p. 6; © Louisiana Travel CC 2.0, p. 7; © OneInchPunch/Shutterstock Images, pp. 8–9; © Paul S. Wolf/Shutterstock Images, p. 8; © Günter Gollnick/ImageBroker/Newscom, p. 9; © Meinzahn/iStock Editorial/Thinkstock, pp. 10–11; © Jim West/ImageBroker/Newscom, p. 11 (left); Historical American Buildings Survey/Library of Congress, p. 11 (right) (HABS LA,17-BATRO,6—28 (CT)); © Jim Hudelson/The Shreveport Times/AP Images, pp. 12–13, 15 (right); © Ioflo69/Shutterstock Images, p. 12 (top); © Pavels Rumme/Shutterstock Images, p. 12 (bottom); © Purcell Team/Alamy, pp. 14–15; © Shreveport-Bossier Convention and Tourist Bureau CC 2.0, p. 15 (left); © Charlie Varley/Sipa Press/Newscom, pp. 16–17; William P. Gottlieb/Library of Congress, p. 16 (LC-GLB13-0456 DLC); © Joyce Marrero/Shutterstock Images, p. 17; © Boykov/Shutterstock Images, pp. 18–19; L. Prang and Co./Library of Congress, p. 19 (top) (LC-DIG-pga-04036); © Jose Gil/Shutterstock Images, p. 19 (bottom); © Melissa Lyttle/Tampa Bay Times/ZumaPress/Newscom, pp. 20–21; © Olivia Perillo CC 2.0, p. 20; Russell Lee/Library of Congress, p. 21 (LC-USF33-011736-M2); © Global Wildlife Center, pp. 22–23; © Anna Hoychuk/Shutterstock Images, p. 22; © Randall R. Saxton CC 2.0, p. 23; © Philip Scalia/Alamy, pp. 24–25; © Ted Drake CC 2.0, pp. 25 (top), 25 (bottom); © nicoolay/iStockphoto, p. 26; © Kenneth Keifer/Shutterstock Images, p. 29 (top); © Lorraine Hudgins/Shutterstock Images, p. 29 (middle left); © Zack Frank/Shutterstock Images, p. 29 (middle right); © Jeffrey M. Frank/Shutterstock Images, p. 29 (bottom).

Front cover: © iStockphoto.com/MSMcCarthy_Photography (Swamp); Carol M. Highsmith's America, Library of Congress LC-DIG-highsm- 11700 (Mardi Gras); JONATHAN BACHMAN/REUTERS/Newscom (Musician); © iStockphoto.com/GatorL (Crawfish); © Laura Westlund/Independent Picture Service (map); © iStockphoto.com/fpm (seal); © iStockphoto.com/vicm (pushpins); © iStockphoto.com/benz190 (cork board).